Everyday
Thai Cooking

Everyday Thai Cooking

EASY, AUTHENTIC RECIPES FROM THAILAND
TO COOK FOR FRIENDS AND FAMILY

SIRIPAN AKVANICH

SPRING HILL

Published by Spring Hill
Spring Hill is an imprint of How To Books Ltd
Spring Hill House, Spring Hill Road, Begbroke
Oxford OX5 1RX, United Kingdom.
Tel: (01865) 375794. Fax: (01865) 379162
info@howtobooks.co.uk
www.howtobooks.co.uk

How To Books greatly reduce the carbon footprint of their books by
sourcing their typesetting and printing in the UK.

British Library Cataloguing in Publication Data.
A catalogue record for this book is available from the British Library.

ISBN 978 1 905862 85 6

Illustrations by Firecatcher Creative
Produced for How To Books by Deer Park Productions, Tavistock
Typeset by Kestrel Data, Exeter, Devon
Printed and bound in Great Britain by Bell & Bain Ltd, Glasgow

NOTE: The material contained in this book is set out in good faith for general
guidance and no liability can be accepted for loss or expense incurred as a result of
relying in particular circumstances on statements made in the book. Laws and
regulations are complex and liable to change, and readers should check the
current position with the relevant authorities before making personal
arrangements.

Dedication

This book is for my mother and grandmother, who cooked for me and taught me how, and for my sons Pom and Pub.

Also for all my Thai food loving *farang* friends: especially Patrick (who initiated the book project and helped with my English) and Sue, and Jack and Silvia.

Contents

Introduction

Let me introduce you to Siripan Akvanich. I do so because, like Winnie-the-Pooh's spelling, her written English can be a bit wobbly. Her cooking, on the other hand, is second to none.

I met Siripan some twenty-five years ago when she was running a small hotel in Thailand's Hua Hin – the town where the King has his summer palace (some of the books I have written have been worked on, in part, sitting in her beachside dining area looking out at the sea). How did this happen? Staying with friends at a resort a hundred metres away along the beach we noticed people walking to her place for dinner. We not only tried it, we loved it, ate there every day and stayed at the hotel the next year – and every year thereafter until the hotel was sold. She became a special friend and we have returned to Hua Hin each year since, sometimes more than once in the year, and Siripan, her family and her cooking have been an important part of every visit.

She made staying at her hotel (and at a guest house she built and ran later) very special. She's capable, amusing and charming – and more important here, she is an excellent cook. Like all Thais, she regards food as very important. Every meal is a significant social occasion and, whether simple or complex, it is essential that what you eat is good. She started to cook when very young and, paraphrasing a little, this is what she told me:

> 'I have been cooking since I was seven years old and began to learn how to cook rice on an old-fashioned charcoal stove. The kitchen was outside the house so that the smoke and smells from the hot stove were kept away from the living areas, and the sizzling chillies didn't make you sneeze. Rice was very difficult to cook; you couldn't go away from the pot and had to stir continuously until the rice was *well done cooked* so that the rice did not stick to the bottom of the pan. If I got it wrong I spent a long time soaking and cleaning the spoilt pan to remove the stuck rice – *I soon*

learned not to do that again. Cooking rice was a regular activity in the early morning before going to school, and rice always went in my lunchbox too. In the evenings after school, even if I was tired, my grandmother taught me to cook Thai desserts.

'In those days there was always rice and it was time-consuming to cook. Now we use an electric steamer and can be busy with other things while the rice cooks. One simple Thai dish, one that can take many forms and is described here, is rice soup, which I love.

'So I have been cooking Thai food ever since I can remember, watching my mum, grandmother and aunties and learning the art of cooking step by step, until I was married with my own kitchen and a family to cook for as a full-time housewife. Then some years later, a big change: I was doing it professionally for both Thais and *farang* (the Thai word for Western foreigners), serving three meals a day at my hotel. But the style of the food was home-cooking and, above all, always *a-roi* (delicious).

'So everything here in my book is a special recipe that I have used throughout my life. The dishes are simple to cook even if you have never tried Thai cooking before. This is healthy food, too, and Thai herbs can, so it is believed, calm a fever or upset stomach and make you feel well.'

I don't know about the medicinal value of Thai food, but many a dish from the land of smiles will put one on your face. Siripan is at pains to make it clear that simplicity is the essence of Thai cooking. You need only basic kitchen ware – a wok, pots, cutting board, sharp knives – and nothing is needed that costs a lot of money. Ingredients, too, are simple: fish, oyster and soy sauce, salt and pepper, curry paste, coconut milk, herbs and . . . but she will come to this.

Everything in the following pages is chosen to be easy and fun to prepare and, most of all, will always be – as Siripan says – *a-roi*.

Enjoy . . .

Patrick Forsyth

Patrick Forsyth has written many non-fiction books including *First Class at last!*, a light-hearted account of a journey through South East Asia, including Thailand; *Beguiling Burma*, about a journey through Burma; and *Smile because it happened*, all about the land of smiles. Find out more www.patrickforsyth.com.

A Little History

When I was at school I learnt something of the history of Thai food.

Over the years, many people have gradually moved into Thailand – from Mongolia, Tibet, India and from China – and across the region people have crossed rivers and mountains to come to our country, bringing their ideas and traditions of food and cooking with them. My school resounded to the sound of many tongues – *Hokien* (still spoken by many in south Thailand), Mandarin and *Tair jeaw* from central Thailand. So some of our herbs and chillies came first from India, noodles came from China, sticky rice from Laos and Cambodia, and Burma too flavoured our curries. All these different influences mixed with Thai traditions to give us the range of food and cooking styles we enjoy today.

Within Thailand, too, there are differences, and as people from the north moved to Bangkok to work they brought their favourite dishes with them (like papaya salad with chicken and distinctive chicken and pork dishes). Thai food is a wondrous mixture and uses the best from everywhere; we even have desserts developed from dishes first made in Spain.

Years ago Thais would eat their meals sitting on the floor, with various dishes served on a tray and eaten with their fingers. Whole families would eat together and I remember meals with my parents, brothers and sisters and grandparents in the old-style Thai wooden house in which we lived. My grandmother lived just next door, the two houses were connected and raised on high posts to protect from floods in the rainy season when rivers, lakes and klongs (canals) overflowed. Fish came to our table from a nearby lake and were always plentiful – so many of them that there were no mosquitoes around; the fish ate all the larvae! Modern ways developed step by step from growing contact with the West, a process started by the Thai King Rama V, until now we use a spoon and fork to eat.

My knowledge and experience of cooking started in those days with lessons from my grandmother (I was the one in the family who enjoyed it – my sister ran away!). She taught me to cook and I have loved doing so ever since. It is easier now, of course. My grandmother had to manage with no refrigerator or rice steamer, but she knew how to create wonderful food and all the dishes I now know and cook stem from a happy childhood that led me to a life of cooking. *Now you can enjoy it too!*

Thai girls
Traditional costumes

The Quick and the Easy

Thai food really is very easy to cook. Thai kitchens reflect this and do not typically have a huge range of equipment. The key thing, used for most of the dishes here, is a wok. Certainly this is best, though you can use a deep frying pan or just a saucepan if necessary; also some recipes use a pot or a steamer. A good wok is designed for fast cooking, the metal bowl is comparatively thin and heat is transferred rapidly. Thais rarely use a non-stick pan, and believe that an old one is better than a new one.

If you have a new wok, then you can 'make it old'. Just coat the whole of the inside with cooking oil, while leaving none pooling in the bottom, and put it on a medium heat for five to six minutes. Because it only contains oil, it will get very hot and may smoke a bit, but that's fine as long as you stop any smoke alarms going off (open a window). Turn off the heat and next rub a whole lot of table salt into the pan (a good-sized wok will need maybe half a cup full). Do this with a thick cloth of some sort as the wok will be hot. Then, with the salt sticking to the pan, again put it on a medium heat, this time for just a little less time, about four or five minutes. When you have done this your wok will be blackened and seasoned and ready to cook in a way that will add to the flavour of the food.

PREPARATION
As you will quickly see as you read on, much of the secret of serving good Thai food is in the preparation, so it pays to have everything ready beforehand.

3

- Have a stock of herbs and spices. You can prepare and store the various sauces and pastes you may want to use (these can be kept for a while in the refrigerator).

- Some dishes use a variety of sauces – say a combination of coconut cream and fish sauce. If so, you can put all this together, in a cup say, at the preparation stage ready just to pour on at the appropriate time.

- Experiment with oils. Sunflower oil is fine, but Thais more often use coconut, peanut, corn or rice oil.

- Have the tools you need ready: knives, spoons and so on.

- Ideally do all the chopping, cutting, grinding and slicing in advance, getting everything ready before you start to cook.

- To make sure everything cooks at the same rate, slice things as appropriate to how long they will need to cook – with a slower-cooking vegetable like carrots being sliced thinnest.

- Because everything is pre-prepared, the recipes give prepared weights, so ¼ cup of chopped shallots means they are measured after you have chopped them.

- Oil the wok before you start, and always make sure that the wok is hot before you start cooking, so you put the ingredients into a hot pan, rather than warming them and the pan together.

- If you need to ensure a dish does not get too dry, then do not overdo the oil, rather add a little stock or water. If you prefer, you can add wine, although wine has been little used in traditional Thai cookery as it is not at its best after a long journey to so hot a country, and importing it has been expensive.

Also note that, while many ingredients mentioned here are available in supermarkets, and certainly from shops specialising in Asian foods, you can save time by buying certain things, like curry paste, ready-made. Even then your approach should be flexible. You may not find the perfect ready-made concoction, but by checking the ingredients and adding a little more of anything that seems needed – more garlic, lemongrass or whatever – you can create just what you like best. Experiment by all means, but then keep a note so that you can reproduce your favourite tastes.

All recipes are set out with measures for four people, though this can, of course, be varied as you wish for larger or smaller portions and more or fewer people.

One specific note is that I use a US cup for measuring. You can use a set of cup measures, which are readily available, or a traditional English cup (tiny variances are not significant), or use an ordinary measuring jug, in which case 1 cup = 250ml.

3

Some Thoughts About Herbs and Spices

In Thailand, we use a lot of spices and some herbs in our cooking and believe that doing so is good for the body and promotes healthy digestion.

Sometimes Thai food can be made hot from herbs like pepper, ginger, galangal, wild ginger and turmeric; or it can be made spicy with chillies (be careful – the smallest ones are usually the hottest). While special chilli pepper can burn your lips and tongue and bring tears to your eyes, we believe that if food is too spicy it is not good for your stomach, and that it spoils a tasty meal. Most Thai food, even if it is spicy, is cooked medium spicy and the level of spiciness is very much a matter of choice (my mother did not like her food too spicy and that is the way I learnt to cook it). If you do not like food too spicy, that's fine, and if you order Thai food in a restaurant and do not want it to burn your tongue, say *mai pet*. Above all, Thai food should be flavoursome.

The most important herbs, spices and flavourings in Thai food include the following:

Hot chilli – *prik ke nu*: The smallest chilli.

Spur chilli – *prik chi fa*: A longer chilli about 13–18cm and either green, red or yellow in colour.

Dried chilli – *prik hang*: A small or large chilli dried in the sun.

Sweet basil 1 – *bai ho ra pa*: An attractive plant with deep green leaves.

Sweet basil 2 – *bai mang rak*: A herb with very light green leaves and a different taste from the standard sweet basil.

Holy basil – *bai kra prao*: With dark green leaves like sweet basil, but a hotter taste.

Lemon basil – *manglak*: This is used as a garnish.

Cardamoms – *luok ka wan*: Dark brown seeds which are aromatic and have a slightly hot taste.

Cinnamon – *ob choiy*: The type grown in South East Asia has brown bark which tends to roll up after being peeled from the branch; it should be roasted to bring out its aroma.

Coriander – *paak chi*: From the parsley family, the leaves, roots and dry seeds are all used in Thai cooking.

Cumin – *yee ra*: A yellow-brown seed that must be roasted before use.

Fish sauce – *nam pla*: A popular flavouring.

Galangal – *ka*: Light-coloured ginger with its own distinctive flavour.

Ginger – *khing*: A light brown ginger rather like galangal but with a distinctive taste.

Wild ginger – *kra chai*: Long yellow-brown roots about 7–12cm long.

Kaffir lime – *ma krood*: Green fruit with a wrinkled skin (the skin or leaves are used in cookery).

Lemon sauce – *naanmanoa*: Used for both desserts and savoury dishes.

Lemongrass – *ta krai*: Grey-green grass with an aromatic smell.

Mint leaves – *bai sa ra nair*: Thai mint has thin leaves that have a round shape.

Palm sugar – *naam tan peeb*: For sweetening.

Pandanus leaf – *bai toiy*: A long, bright leaf like a small palm, which is used in Thai desserts.

Shallot – *hom dang*: A small, round red onion.

Spring shallot – *ton hom*: Onion leaves

Shrimp paste – Kapi: A flavouring paste made from shrimp.

Dried shrimp – *kung haeng*: Sun-dried shrimp used for flavouring.

Tamarind juice – *naam ma kam pak*: Juice extracted from the pods of the tamarind tree.

Turmeric – *Ka min*: A small ginger root with a strong yellow colour inside (the colour can stick on your fingers or your clothes when cutting, so be careful).

MEDICINAL INGREDIENTS
While it would be wrong to promise guaranteed medicinal effects, there are some traditions that have been current for hundreds of years in Thailand, so perhaps they have some validity.

Basil: This is evidently so good for you it is touted as good against infections that are resistant to antibiotics. It is a widely used herb and is also used to create a liquid in which to wash vegetables that might carry unpleasant bacteria.

Chilli: Much used in Thai food, chillies contain capsaicin, which helps to thin the blood and reduce the likelihood of blood clots. Perhaps this means that you are less likely to get DVT (deep vein thrombosis) going home from Thailand after eating lots of Thai food than on your outward journey!

Coconut: This has a high level of fat and calories so you may want to bear that in mind, but coconuts are said to be 'good fats' and likely to lower cholesterol and boost immunity.

Coriander: A seed ubiquitous in many parts of the world, this helps digestion and assists in fighting off infections.

Galangal: This is a close relative of ginger and regarded as the ultimate digestive cure.

Ginger: Known as a digestive, ginger tea (ginger infused in boiling water for ten minutes or so) is prescribed for any kind of stomach problem; it is also believed to alleviate pain.

Lemongrass: This is much used in Thai recipes, not least because it is believed to reduce fevers, diminish headaches and help ward off or shorten the duration of colds and flu.

Mint: An infusion served as a tea is popular, as mint is reputed to help with a wide range of problems from IBS (irritable bowel syndrome) to cancer. And while that claim must be treated with caution, it has a lovely taste and may well do you some good.

Turmeric: This is something you can buy, quite expensively, in capsules in health food shops to help arthritis – it's an anti-inflammatory. It is also believed to help speed up the healing of cuts and wounds and prevent infections. It is much better and less expensive to use some in your cooking.

4

Authentic Thai Cuisine

Ask a Thai which is the main meal of the day and they will tend to say 'all of them'. This is a cookbook, so it sets out to enable you to cook good Thai food, giving you the authenticity that only comes with instructions from an expert. But it is also an introduction to food that is quintessentially Thai, and there are two particular expressions in the Thai language that will help you understand that.

Mai pen rai

If you look up the Thai phrase *mai pen rai* in a dictionary it will say that it means something like 'never mind'. This is rather like saying that the temperature in Thailand is 'rather warm' or that six large whiskies constitutes a 'little drink', thus bringing a whole new meaning to the concept of understatement. The words mean something more like: Never mind – that's life – don't worry – it will all be the same in a hundred years – don't let's waste time dwelling on it – so what's next?

It can be used to put over all or any part of such a sentiment and is a much used and most useful phrase, with no direct counterpart in English that has anything like the same breadth of meaning. The phrase is characteristic of the happy-go-lucky attitude that seems to be so much a part of Thai life.

Why mention this? To give you the confidence to go ahead and try these recipes because they are quick and easy to prepare – and really easy to fix. You should have no disasters, but if something does go wrong, *mai pen rai.* Just have another go, have a drink, chat to your guests . . . and in no time at all you will be sitting down to eat a wonderful meal.

Sanuk

Thai is a difficult language to learn and its pronunciation defies the attempts of many to get their tongues around it. However there is one Thai word that is crucial to understanding and enjoying Thai cuisine: *sanuk.*

Sanuk will usually be translated simply and literally as 'fun'. But it is much more than that: it is an enjoyment of life, of the moment, a putting aside of cares and a concentration on the occasion. The occasion may be something special, though that is not necessary. *Sanuk* best describes the enjoyment of those simple things in life that are pleasurable. It especially describes occasions involving friends and family. And that, of course, includes meals eaten in company and enjoyed together. Cooking and eating are not regarded as refuelling. A meal, whatever it is, must be fun and this is as true of a snack from a mobile kitchen at the roadside (it is said that Thailand is a country where you need to be careful not to be run over by a restaurant) as it is for something more formal. The food being good is important; it adds to the occasion.

And while on the subject of language, I will say that I have given the recipe names in Thai as well as English. Because Thai is written in its own script and is also a tonal language, you will find many different spellings of the English names.

Following the advice here and experiencing the results should be fun. You will not just be able to make a good dish; you will have the beginnings of experiencing real *sanuk* – read on, give it a try . . . and enjoy!

5

Something to Drink

First, something to drink . . .

In Thailand, where the *farang*, such as yourself, might feel it is always hot, we describe having summers as warm, with temperatures of about 36–42°C. A favourite soft drink then is lemon juice with soda, or lemon juice with ice cubes. Our winter it is not really cold like it is in Europe, rather it's about 18–22°C with more windy weather when we like to make a hot drink like ginger tea or lemongrass tea (both of which we believe ward off colds).

benjarong bowl

Lemon Juice
Na manoaw

It is best if you squeeze the lemon juice from the fresh fruit.

SERVES 4

2 cups lemon juice

1 cup water

1 cup syrup (page 25) or honey

Ice cubes

A few lemon slices

* Mix the ingredients together well in a large jug. Keep it cold in the refrigerator.
* Put some ice cubes in a tall glass, pour in the lemon juice and add the lemon slices.

Lemon Soda
Soda manoaw

Again, squeeze the juice from fresh fruit if you can.

SERVES 4

2 cups lemon juice

1 cup soda water

1 cup syrup (page 25)

Ice cubes

A few lemon slices

* Mix all the ingredients together and serve with ice cubes and a slice of lemon.

Iced Lemon Tea
Cha manoaw yen

SERVES 4

1 pot of good English tea

¼ cup lemon juice

¼ cup syrup (page 25)

Ice cubes

A few lemon slices

Here in Thailand, we usually use Lipton's tea, which is regarded by the English as rather weak. Freshly squeezed lemon juice is best.

- Mix the ingredients together and serve with ice cubes and a slice of lemon.

Ginger Tea
Naam kging

SERVES 4

2.5cm piece of fresh root ginger, peeled and thinly sliced or crushed

1 litre water

1–2 tsp sugar

We believe that ginger can reduce fever or a runny nose and assist digestion by reducing gas in the stomach; it is good before travelling too.

- Boil the ginger in the water for 3 minutes.
- Pour into the tea pot, then serve hot with as much sugar as you like.

Lemongrass Tea
Naam tra krai

SERVES 4

4 lemongrass stalks

1 litre water

½ tsp sugar (only if you wish)

We believe that lemongrass keeps warmth in our body, reduces gas in the stomach and also reduces cholesterol levels. And, of course, it has a lovely taste!

- Use only the white part of the lemongrass, crush it and cut it into pieces about 2.5cm long.

- Add the lemongrass to the teapot, pouring on boiling water and leaving to stand for 3 minutes.

- Pour (just like tea) and add some sugar as you like.

Singha Beer
Beer Singha

Cold beer is a traditional accompaniment to Thai food, and *Singha* is the brand of choice for many people. Indeed up until, say, twenty years ago there was no other local beer much in evidence (well probably there was, but its share of the market was tiny).

Singha is named after a mystical lion, one that features in traditional Hindu and Thai stories. The label also features another mythical creature, the winged Garuda, a symbol of Thai royalty and a link to the Royal Warrant granted to the brewers in 1939; indeed Singha's producer, the Boon Rawd Brewery, is the only producer to have this. It is the leading brand, though these days Chang follows as a close second and imported beers, particularly Heineken, sell well too.

All *Singha* beer is brewed in Thailand, so if you buy it elsewhere (and it has been available in the UK since 2009) it will be imported. As part of its promotion in the UK (and elsewhere in Europe) it uses various sporting sponsorships, variously being linked to Chelsea and Manchester United football clubs and the Red Bull Formula One motor racing team. It is a quite strong beer, 5.0%, though its strength was reduced in 2007 from 6.0%. Serve it cold – in Thailand the best restaurants serve it into glasses that have spent some time in the refrigerator – and enjoy!

A tip: when in Thailand's heat, beer warms quickly once served, so many people share a (large) bottle between two people, then order more that will again be cold.

Cheers! Or, as we say in Thailand, *choak dee* (good luck). Now on to the recipes.

Stir-frying and Basic Recipes

The tradition of stir-frying any food in a wok came to Thailand from China. As Chinese people moved into Thailand from the north, they brought with them their experience of growing vegetables everywhere: farm, garden or yard. Vegetables growing in Thailand and China are similar, and Thais copied the Chinese habit of the simple cooking of vegetables stir-fried in a wok and learnt to do the same. Thus this way of cooking – with not too much fat, adding herbs and taking maybe only 10 to 15 minutes to cook on a high heat – soon became the Thai norm. It is easy for you too.

Another important element of Thai cooking is roasting and grinding spices such as cumin and coriander seeds. The flavour will be much more intense if you prepare them yourself just when you need them. Simply toss the seeds in a dry frying pan for a few minutes until they start to release their aroma and turn golden, then remove them at once, leave to cool slightly, and crush in a pestle and mortar.

The recipes in this chapter will form the basis of many of the recipes in the book.

Kaffir lime

¼ cup cooking oil

5–10 garlic cloves, finely chopped

Stir-fried Garlic
Katiam jeaw

This is used with many recipes and can be made and stored in the fridge for a week or so, so that when you cook a dish that needs it all you do is open the jar – and sprinkle on top to enhance the flavour.

- Add the cooking oil to a pan and place over a medium heat.
- Add the garlic and stir for about 3 minutes until it becomes a light gold colour.
- Remove from the heat, strain and allow to cool.
- Store the garlic in a glass jar.

> **Cook's tip**
> Keep the cooking oil to use in dishes that need garlic oil.

Garlic

Steamed Rice
Koa

SERVES 4

4 cups rice

One cup of rice –
that's about 200g – is a
one-person portion,
but you can vary this

You will often need rice to be cooked and ready to serve with your main dishes. I used a steam pot as a child before we had electricity; fortunately cooking rice is now much easier to do. I always use an electric rice cooker. If you don't have one, you'll need to use a heavy-based pan, preferably with a glass lid, over a very low heat, and keep an eye on the rice to make sure it doesn't stick. If you have an automatic electric rice cooker, then you just add the rice and water, then press the 'cook' button.

* Use a medium-sized, deep, non-stick steam pot, about 30cm in diameter or a heavy-based pan. Bring a pan of water to the boil, or boil a kettle of water.

* While the water is heating, wash 2 cups full of rice with 2 cups water. Add the rice to the steamer bowl or the pan, then add the boiling water to cover the rice and come about 2.5cm above the rice.

* Cover tightly and cook the rice on medium to low heat for 20 minutes or until the rice is dry, testing with a fork until it is just as you like.

* Keep the steamed rice warm in the pot until you are ready to serve.

Thai Dipping Sauce
Naam jim

¼ cup fish sauce

¼ cup sliced shallots

2 tbsp lemon sauce

1 tsp red chilli powder

This is not a dish or a meal, just a very tasty addition to many other dishes.

- Pound all the ingredients with a pestle and mortar or blend until finely ground and well mixed.

- Then you are ready to serve the dip with any grilled or barbecued meat dish, or with anything else you find you like it with.

chilli

Massaman Curry Paste
Naam prik kang massaman

Of course you can pick this up ready made when you shop but it is easy to make and will ensure you get exactly the flavour you like – *experiment!*

- Put the chillies, shallots and garlic in a wok and stir-fry for 2 minutes.

- Transfer to a mortar and pound thoroughly to a paste.

- Mix the coriander, lemongrass, shrimp paste, peppers and salt and pound or blend to a paste.

- Put the nutmeg, mace, cloves, cardamom, cumin and coriander in a wok and stir-fry for 2–3 minutes.

- Transfer to the mortar and pound all the ingredients together to a smooth paste.

- Transfer to an airtight jar and store in the refrigerator for up to 2 weeks.

Cook's note
To use a food processor or blender, add a little cooking oil to assist the blending.

MAKES ABOUT 2 CUPS

For the first step

10 large dried chillies, seeded and chopped

½ cup chopped Asian shallots

½ cup chopped garlic cloves

For the second step

1 tsp chopped coriander roots

¼ cup thinly sliced lemongrass stalks, white parts only

1 tsp shrimp paste

1 tsp peppers

½ tsp salt

For the third step

¼ tsp grated nutmeg

¼ tsp blades of mace

¼ tsp whole cloves

¼ tsp cardamom pods

1 tbsp cumin seeds

2 tbsp coriander seeds

15 hot green chillies

3 tbsp chopped shallots

1 tbsp chopped garlic

1 tbsp chopped galangal

1 tbsp chopped lemongrass

½ tbsp chopped kaffir lime zest

½ tbsp chopped coriander root

5 blackpeppercorns

1–3 roasted and ground coriander seeds

½ tbsp roasted and ground cumin seeds

½ tbsp salt

Green Curry Paste
Nam prik kang keaw wan

Some recipes, like the green curries, need green curry paste. You can buy this easily and conveniently in a supermarket, of course, but it's easy to make and this recipe guarantees that what you use will then be authentically Thai.

- Pound all the ingredients with a pestle and mortar or blend until finely ground. *Then you are ready to make your authentic Thai curry!*

Lemongrass

Mild Green Curry Paste
Naamprikkang

This is milder paste so is a good one to start with if you are not sure how hot you like your food.

- Using a pestle and mortar and adding the ingredients one at a time, pound the lemongrass, garlic, Asian shallots, salt, kaffir lime zest, coriander roots, galangal, shrimp paste and pepper until smooth.

- Add the green chillies and continue pounding to create a smooth paste.

- Transfer from the mortar to an airtight jar and store in the refrigerator for up to 2 weeks.

> **Cook's note**
> To use a food processor or blender, add some cooking oil to assist the smooth blending.

2 lemongrass stalks, white part only, thinly sliced

4–5 garlic cloves, thinly sliced

3 Asian shallots, thinly sliced

½ tsp salt

1 tsp finely chopped kaffir lime zest

3–5 finely chopped coriander roots

1–3 pieces galangal, thinly sliced

1 tbsp shrimp paste

½ tsp ground black pepper

8–10 large green chillies, seeded and cut into thin strips

Red Curry Paste
Naam prik kang ped

5 large dried chillies, seeded and sliced lengthways

2 lemongrass stalks, white part only, thinly sliced

3–5 garlic cloves, finely chopped

3–4 Asian shallots, finely chopped

2–3 pieces galangal, thinly sliced

1 tsp chopped kaffir lime zest

1 tsp chopped coriander root

1 tsp shrimp paste

½ tsp ground black pepper

½ tsp salt

♦ Soak the chillies in hot water for 3 minutes until soft.

♦ Using a pestle and mortar, pound the lemongrass, garlic, Asian shallots, galangal, kaffir lime zest and coriander roots until you have a smooth paste.

♦ Drain the chillies and add them to the paste with the shrimp paste, pepper and salt, then pound everything together until you create a fine, smooth paste.

♦ Transfer to an airtight jar and keep in the refrigerator for up to 2 weeks.

Cook's note

If you use a food processor or blender, add some cooking oil to assist smooth blending.

Soya Milk
Naam toa hu

MAKES ABOUT 6 LITRES

1kg soya beans, cracked

If your diet allows, you can add fresh cows' milk to the soya milk to make a mixture.

- Place the beans in a large pan, cover with hot water and leave to soak for 3 hours.

- Mash the soya beans into the water, then pour into a sieve lined with muslin and allow the soya milk to drain off.

- Put the liquid in a clean pan on low heat and stir all the time for 30 minutes.

- Serve like hot milk with a spoonful of syrup stirred in to taste.

Cook's note

Make syrup by dissolving a cup of sugar in a cup of water, then boiling for a few minutes until just golden.

7

4 cups water

400g skinless chicken breast,cut into 2.5cm dice

1 large potato, peeled and cut into 2.5cm dice

200g tomatoes, quartered

¼ cup light soy sauce

1 tbsp chopped fresh coriander

Soups

thai Orchid

Chicken Soup
Soup kai

This is a good, tasty traditional soup. It can be made more hot and spicy to taste: just add the some lemon juice and some small chillies.

* Bring the water to the boil, then turn the heat to low. Add the chicken and cook for 4 minutes.

* Add the potatoes and cook for 3 minutes.

* Add the tomatoes and soy sauce and cook for about 5 minutes or until the chicken is well cooked.

* Serve sprinkled with coriander.

Tofu Soup
Toam jurd toa hu

Tofu came to Thailand from China with the influx of Chinese immigrants. This soup is popular because it has a good flavour, somewhere between traditional Thai and Chinese food. It has been served, usually with rice, in Thailand for more than a hundred years. In Thailand, tofu is sold in 225g rolls, and you need one per person. You can serve this soup European style as a starter, or stir in rice to make a more substantial dish.

- Bring the stock to the boil over a medium heat.

- Mix the pork or chicken mince with the garlic and pepper and shape into small balls. Drop into the stock and cook on a low heat for 10 minutes until the chicken or pork is well cooked.

- Raise the heat to medium, add the tofu and soy sauce and cook for 2 more minutes.

- Add the spring onion and fried garlic on the top and serve in soup bowls.

Cook's note

You can make your own stock or use a stock cube, using 1 cube for 4 cups boiling water.

SERVES 4

4 cups chicken stock

300g pork or chicken mince

1 tsp chopped garlic

½ tsp ground black pepper

4 x 225g rolls of white tofu cake, cut into 2.5cm cubes

2 tbsp light soy sauce

¼ cup chopped spring onion

To garnish
A little stir-fried garlic (page 18)

4 cups water

¼ cup cooking oil

4 eggs

¼ cup soy sauce

2 tbsp chopped spring onion

1 tbsp stir-fried garlic (page 18)

Egg Soup
Toam jurd kgai

- Bring the water to the boil in a saucepan.

- Add the cooking oil to a frying pan and place on a medium heat.

- Break the eggs into a bowl and beat thoroughly.

- Add the eggs to the oil in the pan and cook for about 4 minutes like an omelette, gently tipping the pan to allow the mixture to run underneath and set, then turning to cook until both sides are light gold in colour and beginning to go crispy.

- Cut the egg into strips and add to the water with the soy sauce and spring onion.

- Serve in soup bowls garnished with stir-fried garlic.

Glass Noodle Soup
Tom jurd woonsen

You can make this soup with pork or chicken.

- Cover the noodles in water and soak for about 20 minutes until soft.

- Put the chicken stock or instant soup in a pot and boil for 3 minutes.

- Roll the minced pork into small meatballs, add to the stock and cook for 3 minutes until well done.

- Drain the glass noodles, add the them to the pan and cook on a low heat for 3 minutes.

- Add the soy sauce, spring onions and cook for 3 minutes.

- Spoon into individual bowls and sprinkle with stir-fried garlic and pepper to serve.

SERVES 4

3 x 25g packs glass noodles

4 cups chicken stock or instant soup

300g minced pork

6 tbsp light soy sauce

2 bunches of spring onions, cut into 5cm long strips

1 tbsp chopped stir-fried garlic (page 18)

Freshly ground black pepper

Ayutthaya Elephant Camp

5 Asian shallots

1 tsp shrimp paste

2–5 coriander roots, chopped

8 black or white peppercorns

3 cups water

¼ cup tamarind juice

3 tbsp fish sauce

2 tbsp palm sugar

1kg white snapper fillets, cut into 5cm slices

2 tbsp thinly sliced young ginger root

3 spring onions, cut into 5cm long pieces

To garnish

¼ cup chopped coriander leaves

Sweet and Sour White Snapper Soup
Tom som plakrapong koaw

If you cannot buy white snapper, use any firm-fleshed white fish.

- Pound together the shallots, shrimp paste, coriander roots and peppercorns until they are well blended.

- Put into a pan over a medium heat and add the water, the tamarind juice, fish sauce and palm sugar, bring to the boil and boil for 3 minutes.

- Add the fish meat and cook for 3 minutes.

- Stir in the ginger and spring onions to give a sweet and sour flavour.

- Garnish with coriander leaves, serve with steamed rice.

Won Ton Soup
Keiw nam

Another tasty soup, you can vary the amount of garlic in this dish to taste.

- Mix the minced prawns with the soy sauce, coriander root and chopped garlic and season with pepper.

- Place 1 tsp of this mixture into the middle of each won ton sheet, gather up and squeeze the corners together to make little 'purses'.

- Bring the stock to the boil, add the light soy sauce and the won ton and cook for 2–3 minutes.

- Serve sprinkled with the chopped spring onion, coriander and stir-fried garlic.

200–300g prawn mince

1 tbsp soy sauce

1 tbsp chopped coriander root

1 tbsp finely chopped garlic

Freshly ground black pepper

20 square wan ton sheets

8 cups chicken stock

¼ cup light soy sauce

2 tbsp chopped spring onion

1 tbsp chopped fresh coriander

1 tbsp stir-fried garlic (page 18)

1kg tender beef

4 tbsp cooking oil

1 tbsp butter

500g small tomatoes, diced

2 large onions, diced

1–2 bay leaves

¼ cup light soy sauce

6 cups water

1 large potato, peeled and diced

1 tbsp Worcestershire sauce

Beef Soup

Soup nour

My friend Patrick, who helped me to write the book, says this is one of his favourites as it has a 'unique and special taste'. The soup is usually made so that the beef taste is just a little bit salty and sour.

♦ Cut the beef into long strips and then into small dice.

♦ Heat the oil and butter in a wok over a medium heat for 1–3 minutes until hot.

♦ Add the tomatoes and onion and stir-fry for 5 minutes until the vegetables are soft and the tomato sauce is red and oily.

♦ Add the beef, bay leaves and soy sauce and stir everything together.

♦ Add the water, turn the heat down to low, and simmer for 30 minutes. Adding a little more boiling water during cooking if necessary.

♦ Add the potatoes and cook for 15 minutes until the potatoes are soft.

♦ Add the Worcestershire sauce and serve.

Spicy Mushroom Soup
Tom yam hed

You can give this soup a sharper taste if you like by adding more salt, more lemon or more chilli.

- Bring the water to the boil in a pan over a medium heat and boil for 3 minutes.

- Add the mushrooms, lemongrass, kaffir lime leaves, chillies, galangal, soy sauce and lemon juice and cook for another 3 minutes.

Serve. *Easy, all done.*

SERVES 4

4 cups water

1kg any fresh mushrooms, diced

3 lemongrass stalks, white part only, cut into 5cm pieces

4–6 kaffir lime leaves

3–5 small chillies, chopped

4–5 pieces galangal

¼ cup soy sauce

¼ cup lemon juice

kaffir lime

6 cups chicken stock

500g chicken breast

6 cups water

500g beansprouts

1kg fresh flat rice
noodles

1 tbsp garlic oil

2 tbsp chopped spring
onions

2 tbsp chopped fresh
coriander

3 tbsp soy sauce

Chicken Noodle Soup
Kuay teaw naam kai

You can use fresh or dried noodles but you'll need to cook
dried noodles first. You can make your own chicken stock
by boiling any bones with some vegetables in water for
20 minutes.

* Sprinkling of chilli powder or chopped chillies in
  vinegar

* Bring the stock to the boil, add the chicken breast
  and cook for 15 minutes on a low heat.

* Lift the chicken out of the stock with a slotted spoon
  and cut into thin slices. Keep the stock warm.

* Meanwhile put the water and beansprouts in
  another pan, leave to soak for 3 minutes, then bring
  to the boil and simmer for 20 minutes. Drain.

* Add the noodles to the stock and soak for 3 minutes.
  Stir in a little cooking oil.

* Spoon the noodles into serving bowls with the
  garlic oil, beansprouts, chicken breast, spring onion,
  chopped coriander and soy sauce. Spoon over
  the chicken stock. Serve sprinkled with dry chilli
  powder or chillies in vinegar if you like a more spicy
  taste.

Thai Vegetable Soup
Kang raing

SERVES 4

A bottle gourd or Asian gourd (*buab*) – sometimes called a calabash or bottle squash – is green, long and slender with a tough striped skin (rather like courgette); it needs to be peeled before cooking.

- Put the shallots, shrimp paste, dried shrimp, peppercorns and salt into a blender or food processor and blend until smooth.

- Bring the water to the boil on a medium heat, and boil for 3 minutes.

- Add the pumpkin and courgette or squash and continue cooking for 3 more minutes.

- Add the corn, mushrooms, prawns and fish sauce and cook for a further 3 minutes.

- Serve hot, garnished with lemon basil.

2–3 shallots, thinly sliced

1 tbsp shrimp paste

1 tbsp dried shrimps

½ tbsp black peppercorns

1 tsp salt

6 cups water

200g pumpkin, peeled, seeded and diced

200g bottle squash or courgette, peeled and diced

100g baby corn, diced

100g straw mushrooms, halved

250g fresh prawns, peeled and deveined

2 tbsp fish sauce

1 tbsp chopped fresh lemon basil

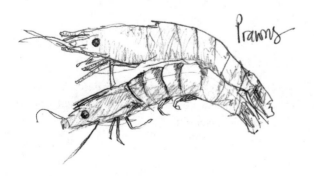

Prawns

8

Salads

Thai salads are very different from Western salads. They can be hot and spicy – very good to enjoy with cold beer or a Thai whisky . . . which is hot! hot! You can drink more to kill the spiciness, but be careful not to get drunk!

SERVES 4

4 long cucumbers

1 large carrot, peeled

200g small red tomatoes, quartered

4 Asian shallots, thinly sliced

½ tsp salt

½ tsp sugar

4 tbsp lemon juice

4 lettuce leaves

½ cup dried shrimp

Cucumber Salad
Yaam tang kwa

Do not use rocket leaves for your salad – the taste is not good with Thai food.

- Slice the cucumber and carrot into long strips to look like noodles; a vegetable-peeler style serrated knife does this well.

- Put all the vegetables in a bowl and stir to mix, adding the salt, sugar and lemon juice.

- Place the lettuce leaves on to the plates, then put the salad mixture on top and sprinkle with dried shrimp before serving.

Wing Bean Salad with Prawns
Yaam tuo plu

This has a lovely spicy taste, but if you like an even more spicy flavour you can add some chilli powder – but be careful!

Wing beans can be bought in Asian supermarkets, but if you can't find them, use green beans or sugar snap peas instead.

- First, make the dressing. Heat coconut cream, fish sauce, lemon juice, palm sugar and Thai chilli oil on a medium heat for 3 minutes, then allow to cool.

- Then stir-fry the shallots on a medium heat in a little of the cooking oil for about 3 minutes until they become light brown in colour. Remove from the heat and leave to cool and keep for the garnish.

- Bring a pan of salted water to the boil, add the wing beans and boil for 3–4 minutes. Drain, cool in cold water, then slice very thinly and place in a bowl.

- Boil the prawns in hot water for 3–4 minutes, then drain, cool and add to the bowl. Toss in the dressing and garnish with the stir-fried shallots and peanuts.

SERVES 4

½ cup coconut cream

2 tbsp fish sauce

6 tbsp lemon juice

½ tsp palm sugar

2 tbsp Thai chilli oil

½ cup chopped Asian shallots

6 tbsp cooking oil

Salt

500g wing beans or snake beans, cut into 7.5cm pieces

12 prawns, peeled and halved

To garnish

5 small red chillies, to garnish

4 tbsp crushed peanuts

chilli

Thai Prawn Salad with Herbs
Pla koong

SERVES 4

4 tbsp fish sauce

6 tbsp lemon juice

500g medium prawns, peeled and finely chopped

10 lemongrass stalks, white part only, thinly sliced

8 Asian shallots, very thinly sliced

To garnish

20–30 fresh mint leaves

1 small chilli, finely chopped

Here is a dish with a sweet and sour flavour. The taste of prawn salad should be medium spicy, but you can strengthen the taste as you like.

- Stir together the fish sauce and lemon juice and mix well to make a sauce.

- Put this sauce into a pan with the prawns and place on a medium heat for 3–5 minutes, stir-frying until the prawns are cooked.

- Remove from the heat and leave to cool.

- When cool, add the lemongrass and shallots and mix everything together.

- Serve on to plates and garnish with the mint leaves and chillies.

Glass Noodle Salad
Yaam woon sen

SERVES 4

3 x 25g packs of glass noodles

1 cup thinly sliced onions

1 cup small tomatoes

1–2 small chillies, chopped

2 tbsp soy sauce

¼ lemon juice

¼ cup soy sauce

A few green salad leaves

Use whichever salad leaves you prefer, although rocket is not good with Thai food. You can add more lemon juice or a little salt to suit your taste.

◆ Soak the noodles in water for about 20 minutes until soft, then drain and cut in half.

◆ Bring a pot of water to the boil, add the glass noodles and boil for 2–3 minutes.

◆ Drain the noodles and place in a bowl with the onions, tomatoes, chillies, fish sauce, lemon juice and soy sauce and toss together.

◆ Serve on top of the green salad leaves.

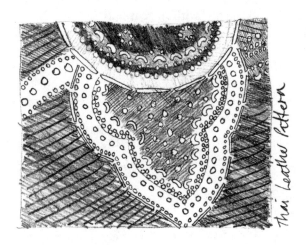

Thai Leather Pattern

Glass Noodle Salad with Prawns
Yaam woon sen koong

2 x 40g packs of glass noodles

300g medium prawns, peeled

2 red chillies, finely diced

6 tbsp lemon juice

4 tbsp fish sauce

1 tsp sugar

10 red shallots, thinly sliced

½ cup chopped spring onion

2 medium tomatoes, diced

5–6 coriander leaves

- Soak the noodles in water for about 20 minutes until soft, then drain.

- Bring a pot of water to the boil, add the glass noodles and boil for 2–3 minutes until soft. Drain and cut into pieces 7–10cm long and place into cold water.

- Boil the prawns in water for 3–4 minutes, then remove and leave to cool.

- To make the salad dressing, place the chillies, lemon juice, fish sauce and sugar in a bowl and mix together. Stir in the cold prawns and the noodles, the shallots, spring onion and tomatoes. Pour over the dressing and toss together.

- Serve garnished with the coriander.

Prawn Salad
Pla kung

The taste of this prawn salad should be medium strength but you can add more chillies to create a spicier taste, or leave out the chillies if that's how you like your salad.

- Cut the heads off the prawns and cut along the back, remove the intestinal thread and open them up, keeping them joined along the base and tail.

- Mix 3 tbsp of the lemon juice with the fish sauce, Thai chilli oil, palm sugar and chillies.

- Heat a small pan on medium heat, add the prawns with the remaining lemon juice and stir-fry quickly for 2 minutes.

- Remove from the heat and add the chilli oil mixture, the lemongrass, shallots and half the mint leaves.

- Spoon on to the salad leaves and serve sprinkled with the remaining mint.

SERVES 4

16 prawns

5 tbsp lemon juice

2 tbsp fish sauce

2 tbsp Thai chilli oil

1 tbsp palm sugar

1–2 small chillies, chopped (omit these if it makes it too spicy)

½ cup very thinly sliced lemongrass stalks, white part only

½ cup thinly sliced Asian shallots

½ cup chopped mint leaves

4 green salad leaves

1kg chicken mince

5 tbsp lemon juice

4–6 tbsp fish sauce

½ cup uncooked rice

1 cup chopped shallots

½ spring onion, chopped

½ tsp chilli powder

½ cup chopped fresh mint leaves

Chicken Salad
Laab kai

You can also serve this salad with some fresh vegetables to make larger portions and add to the great flavours.

- Put the chicken mince, lemon juice and fish sauce in a pot on medium heat and stir-fry for 4–5 minutes.

- Cook the rice in another pan for a few minutes on medium heat until it is light gold colour, then grind in a blender or with a pestle and mortar.

- Add the rice to the chicken, stir together and leave to cool.

- Mix in the shallots, chilli powder and spring onion and serve garnished with mint leaves.

Mint

Mixed Salad with Peanut Dressing
Yaam yai

If you want the dressing a little spicier, then add one small chilli.

- First, make the dressing. Blend all dressing ingredients together on medium speed in a blender or with a pestle and mortar.

- Then gently mix together the lettuce, cucumber and onions. Toss with the dressing and arrange on serving plates. Top with the chicken, tomatoes and finally the carrots to finish.

For the dressing

½ cup rice vinegar

1–3 garlic cloves, chopped

4 tbsp palm sugar

½ tsp salt

3 tbsp roasted peanuts

For the salad

500g lettuce leaves, cut into 5–7cm long pieces

200g onions, thinly sliced

100g small cucumbers, peeled and thinly sliced

200g cooked chicken breast, cut into very thin 5–7cm long pieces

300g tomatoes, sliced

100g carrots, peeled and thinly sliced or grated

Garlic

4 pieces pork steak

8 lemongrass stalks, white part only, very thinly sliced

½ cup thinly sliced shallots

4–6 tbsp fish sauce

6 tbsp lemon juice

½ tsp sugar

6 small dried chillies, roasted or stir-fried in the pan

½ tsp chilli powder

½ cup chopped fresh mint leaves

Fresh mixed vegetables for serving

2 long cucumbers, thinly sliced

200g snake beans, washed and cut into 13 15cm long pieces

1 medium Chinese cabbage, quartered

Roasted Pork Salad
Yaam moo yang

The snake beans used in this recipe can be found in Asian stores, or you can substitute green beans or sugar snap peas.

♦ Preheat the oven to 180°C/gas 4 and roast the pork in the oven for 20 minutes, then slice thinly.

♦ Put the pork in a bowl and add the lemongrass and shallots.

♦ Mix the fish sauce, lemon juice and sugar to make the dressing, pour over the salad and toss together.

♦ Sprinkle with roasted chillies, chilli powder and mint leaves on top to finish. Serve with the fresh vegetables.

Aubergine Salad
Yaam makour yaow

- Preheat the oven to 160°C/gas 3 and roast the aubergines in the oven for 30 minutes so that they become brown.

- Soak in cold water until cool, then peel and cut into 7.5cm long strips.

- Place the roasted aubergines on serving plates with the eggs and shallots.

- Mix all the ingredients for the dressing in a small bowl, then spoon over the salad and sprinkle with the chillies, garlic, dried shrimp and mint.

8 long aubergines

2 hard-boiled eggs, quartered

5 shallots, thinly sliced

For the dressing

4 tbsp fish sauce

6 tbsp lemon juice

To garnish

1–2 small red or green chillies, finely chopped

8 garlic cloves, finely chopped

2–4 cups dried shrimp, rinsed and dried

10–12 fresh mint leaves, finely chopped

Thai Elephant figurine

Mixed Seafood Salad
Yaam talay

200g mixed seafood,
a selection of different
seafoods such as
prawns, mussels,
squid and fish

1 large onion. thinly
sliced

1–3 tomatoes, sliced
into pieces about 1cm
thick

4 sticks of Chinese
celery, cut into 5cm
long pieces

For the salad dressing

2 tbsp chopped garlic

4 tbsp fish sauce

6 tbsp lemon juice

1 tbsp syrup or palm
sugar

5 garlic cloves,
chopped

To garnish

5 small chillies, any
colour, finely chopped

1 tbsp chopped fresh
coriander

Chinese celery is more delicate than the Western variety
with crisp, hollow stems. You can leave it out if you cannot
buy it where you are.

- Blanch the seafood in boiling water for 30 seconds,
  then drain.

- Place all the seafood in a bowl and add the onion
  and tomatoes.

- Mix together all the salad dressing ingredients, then
  pour over the salad and stir together.

- Add the Chinese celery and stir well to mix.

- Spoon on to plates and sprinkle with chilli and
  coriander to garnish.

Garlic

Coconut Rice with Papaya Salad
Koa maan somtaam

- Put the rice, coconut cream and salt in an electric rice cooking pot and cook until done.

- If you are cooking in a pan, use a non-stick pan and make sure the coconut cream covers the rice by 2.5cm. Cook on a low heat for about 20 minutes, stirring, until the rice is soft and dry.

- When the rice is well done, stir just a little and then set aside to keep warm until you are ready to serve.

- Mix together the papaya, tomatoes and green beans on serving plates.

- Blend the garlic with the dried shrimp, fish sauce and palm sugar. Add the half the lemon juice, then taste and add more if you want – it should be sour and sweet.

- Pour over the salad and spoon the coconut rice on to the serving plates.

For the rice

2 cups jasmine rice

3 cups coconut cream

½ tsp salt

For the salad

1kg green papaya, peeled and cut into long strips to look like noodles

200g small tomatoes, quartered

200g long green beans cut 5cm long pieces

For the dressing

4 garlic cloves

2 tbsp small dried shrimps

¼ cup fish sauce

2 tbsp palm sugar

¼ cup lemon juice

2–4 green salads leaves

coconut

Minced Pork Salad with Herbs
Laab moo

4 tbsp rice

500g minced pork

100ml lemon juice

½ cup shallot, thinly sliced

6 tbsp fish sauce

½ cup thinly sliced shallots

½ cup chopped spring onion

1 tsp ground chilli

To garnish

½ cup chopped fresh mint leaves

Side salad

You can also make this salad with chicken, in which case it is called laab kai.

- ◆ Stir the rice in a pan on a low heat for about 3 minutes until it is golden brown, then grind in a food processor for 2 minutes.

- ◆ Heat a wok on a medium heat, add the pork, lemon juice and fish sauce and cook for 3 minutes.

- ◆ Remove from the heat and add the toasted and ground rice, the shallots, spring onion and ground chilli and mix well.

- ◆ Garnish with mint leaves and serve on individual plates with side salad.

Mint

Steamed Dishes

You can use any kind of steamer for these recipes, whether you have an electric steamer, a metal or bamboo one – or even a metal colander over a pan of boiling water.

Steamed Fish Cake
Hor moak

- Mix the coconut cream with the curry paste, eggs and fish sauce, then add the fish and mix well.

- Put the fish mixture in the steamer and cook for 20–25 minutes on medium heat until the fish cake sets firm; then it's ready for serving.

- Place the Chinese cabbage at the bottom of serving bowls, top with the fish cake and add the basil leaves and chillies on the top.

4 cups coconut cream

2 tbsp red curry paste (page 24)

2 eggs

2–4 tbsp fish sauce

1–2kg any fish fillets you fancy, sliced

1 Chinese cabbage, cut each leaf into 4

1 sprig of sweet basil, leaves only

2–3 large red chillies, very thinly sliced

Steamed Fish with Soy Sauce

Pla noung se eiw

2kg white fish fillets

4 tbsp soy sauce

2 tbsp sesame oil

30g fresh root ginger, peeled and sliced

200g any mushrooms, quartered

2 rashers of bacon, cut into 2.5cm long pieces

1 bunch of spring onions, cut into 5cm long pieces

- Cook the fish in a steamer for 5 minutes, then lift out the fish, reserving the fish stock.

- Warm a pan over a high heat, then stir-fry the soy sauce, sesame oil, ginger, mushrooms and bacon.

- Pour the sauce on the top of the fish and place in the steamer. Cover and steam for 30 minutes on a medium heat.

- Serve sprinkled with the spring onion on top.

Ginger

Steamed Fish with Lemon Sauce

Pla noung manoa

- Heat the steamer on a high heat for 5 minutes, then use a medium heat to steam the fish for about 25 minutes until cooked, then remove the fish stock.

- Mix together the sauce ingredients: lemon juice, garlic, fish sauce, sugar and chillies and *use soon!*

- Arrange the fish on serving plates, spoon over the lemon sauce, garnish with the lemon slices along the plate and it's all ready to serve.

2kg any fish fillets, sliced

For the lemon sauce
½ cup lemon juice

½ cup finely chopped garlic

2 tbsp fish sauce

1 tbsp sugar

1–3 small chillies, chopped

To garnish
2 lemons, thinly sliced

benjarong bowl

Steamed Eggs with Onion and Prawn

Kgai toon koong

4 eggs

½ cup water

1 tbsp soy sauce

100g chopped prawns

1 onion, chopped

1 tbsp finely chopped spring onion

1 tbsp stir-fried garlic (page 18)

This recipe is best cooked in a steamer.

- Warm the steam pot on a high heat for 15 minutes, then turn the heat to low.

- Break the eggs into a bowl and stir with a fork for 10 seconds, adding the water, soy sauce, prawns and onion and mixing well.

- Put all the ingredients into the steamer on a low heat, then sprinkle the spring onions and stir-fried garlic on the top. Steam for 15–20 minutes or until the eggs are well set.

Sea Mussels with Lemongrass
Hoy mang poo ob

SERVES 4

- Place the mussels, lemongrass, shallots, water, salt, basil leaves and kaffir lime leaves in a large pan. Cover with a lid and put on a high heat to cook for 5 minutes or until the mussel shells open.

- Remove from the heat, discarding any that remain closed.

- Keep the mussels warm in the pot and serve them with Thai seafood sauce for diners to dip the mussels in.

2kg mussels, scrubbed and bearded

500g lemongrass stalks, white part only, cut into 7.5cm pieces

5 shallots, chopped

6 cups water

½ tsp salt

3 sprigs of sweet basil leaves

10 kaffir lime leaves

To serve

Thai seafood sauce (page 54)

½ cup chopped garlic

3 tbsp palm sugar

½ tsp salt

2 large green chillies, seeded

2 small green chillies

½ cup vinegar

Thai Seafood Sauce
Naam jim talay

This tasty sauce can be served with any seafood dish to make it special.

◆ Put all the ingredients in a bowl and blend until it is all well mixed.

Garlic

Stir-fried Dishes

Thai girls Traditional costumes

Fish with Celery
Pla paad kurn chai

- With the wok on a medium heat, add ¼ cup of the cooking oil and fry the fish until it becomes light brown. Transfer to a serving plate and keep it warm.

- Add the remaining cooking oil to the wok and, still on medium heat, stir in the garlic, onions, soy sauce, water and celery and cook for just 3 minutes.

- Spoon the sauce over the fish, garnish with chillies and serve with steamed rice.

½ cup cooking oil

1kg white snapper meat, cut thickly into 2.5cm pieces

1 tbsp chopped garlic

2 large onions, sliced

¼ cup soy sauce

¼ cup water

200g celery, cut into 5cm long pieces

2 large red chillies, thinly sliced

To serve
Steamed rice (page 19)

2 large cucumbers

1kg tomatoes

2 onions

¼ cup cooking oil

1–2 garlic cloves,
finely chopped

2 tsp soy sauce or 1
tsp fish sauce

½ tsp sugar, or to
taste

¼ cup water
(optional)

½ spring onion, cut
into 5cm pieces

To serve
Steamed rice
(page 19)

Stir-fried Vegetables in Sweet and Sour Sauce
Paad pak peaw wan

Sometimes we buy lots of vegetables for cooking but don't ever use them; we put them in the refrigerator and maybe throw them away later. But you can make stir-fried vegetables with a mixture, even of what is left – *I make it with whatever is cheapest on the day!* Today, imagine you have some cucumber, tomatoes and onion and we'll cook them with a little sweet and sour sauce. Serve this with almost any other dish.

- Cut the cucumbers, tomatoes and onions into even-sized pieces – they can be any size and shape you like.

- Heat the cooking oil to a medium heat in a wok and cook the garlic first for a few minutes until it is fragrant.

- Add the tomatoes and stir-fry quickly until cooked.

- Add the cucumbers and onions, the soy sauce and the sugar, if you like. Stir everything together for 3–4 minutes, adding a little water if necessary.

- Stir in the spring onion.

- Transfer to a serving dish and serve with steamed rice.

Cook's tip
Increasing the quantity of tomatoes will give more of a tomato sauce base to the dish (and fresh tomatoes do this so much better than a bottled or canned sauce).

Stir-fried Mixed Vegetables with Prawns
Paad paak roam koong

SERVES 4

For this dish, you can use a selection of mixed vegetables, such as baby corn, carrot, snow bean and broccoli.

- Cook all vegetables in boiling salted water for thirty seconds, then drain and plunge into iced water to await the next stage.

- Add the cooking oil to the wok and heat until hot. Add the garlic and cook on a medium heat for a few minutes until light gold colour.

- Add the prawns and stir-fry for 3–4 minutes until cooked.

- Drain the vegetables from the iced water, add them to the pan and stir-fry for 3 minutes until hot.

- Add the soy sauce and stir-fry for 2–3 minutes until well mixed.

- Spoon on to serving dish and drizzle a little garlic oil on the top to finish.

100g baby corn, chopped

1 large carrot, peeled and cut into long thin slices

500g snow beans, peeled

1 large head of broccoli, divided into florets

Salt

½ cup cooking oil

1–3 garlic cloves, thinly sliced

300g prawns, peeled and cut open along the back

½ cup soy sauce

A little garlic oil

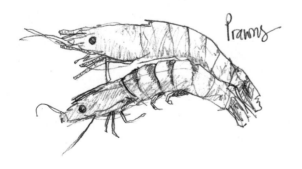

Prawns

Stir-fried Mixed Vegetables with Chicken
Paad paak roam kai

100g baby corn, chopped

1 large carrot, peeled and cut into long thin slices

500g snow beans, peeled

1 large head of broccoli, divided into florets

Salt

½ cup cooking oil

1–3 garlic cloves, thinly sliced

200g chicken breast, sliced into long, thin 6cm pieces

½ cup soy sauce

A little garlic oil

- Cook all vegetables in boiling salted water for thirty seconds, then drain and plunge into iced water to await the next stage.

- Add the cooking oil to the wok and heat until hot. Add the garlic and cook on a medium heat for a few minutes until light gold colour.

- Add the chicken and stir-fry for 3–4 minutes until cooked.

- Drain the vegetables from the iced water, add to the pan and stir-fry for 3 minutes until hot.

- Add the soy sauce and stir-fry for 2–3 minutes until well mixed.

- Spoon on to serving dish and drizzle a little garlic oil on the top to finish.

Stir-fried Vegetables with Crispy Bacon
Paad paak becon krob

SERVES 4

- Cook the bacon in a hot wok for a few minutes until golden and crisp. Remove from the wok.

- Add the cooking oil to the wok over a medium heat and stir-fry the vegetables and garlic for 2 minutes.

- Add the water, then the soy sauce and stir-fry for 2–3 minutes.

- Spoon on to plates and sprinkle the crispy bacon on the top to finish.

300g bacon, cut into 1cm chunks

¼ cup cooking oil

300g Chinese kale, cut into 5cm long pieces

2–3 garlic cloves, chopped

¼ cup water

2–4 tbsp soy sauce

Grand Palace of Thailand Bangkok

Stir-fried Aubergine
Paad makour yao

500g aubergine

¼ cup cooking oil

1 tbsp chopped garlic

300g red tomatoes,
thinly sliced

300g pork or chicken
mince

½ cup water

½ cup basil leaves

1–2 large red chillies,
finely chopped

4 tbsp fish sauce

½ tbsp palm sugar

- Cut the aubergines into 2cm dice and blanch in boiling water for about 30 seconds, then transfer to cold water.

- Heat the cooking oil in the wok over a medium heat and when it is hot, add the garlic, tomatoes and mince and stir-fry for 3–4 minutes. Add a little water if the mixture becomes dry.

- Add the basil leaves and chillies and cook for 2 minutes.

- Remove from the heat. Add the aubergines. fish sauce and sugar and stir until well mixed. Spoon on to the plates – it's ready.

Thai Pea Aubergines

Fried Chicken with Basil Leaves

Paad kapoa kai

SERVES 4

- Blend the garlic with the chillies.

- On a medium heat add the cooking oil to the wok, then add the chillies and chopped garlic. Stir in the wok for just 30 seconds.

- Add the chicken mince and stir in the soy sauce and sugar. Cook for about 5 minutes until the chicken is well cooked.

- Add the basil leaves, stir quickly for just 30 seconds and it will be ready to serve.

4 garlic cloves, chopped

4 large chillies of mixed colours, chopped

¼ cup cooking oil

500g chicken mince

2–4 tbsp soy sauce

½ tbsp palm sugar

½ cup sweet basil leaves

Cardamom

Prawns with Lemon Sauce

Koong tod manao

2 eggs

Salt

8 large prawns

1 cup cooking oil

2–4 cups breadcrumbs

3–4 cups lemon juice

3–4 cups palm sugar

2 lemons, thinly sliced

To make the lemon sauce, you need equal quantities of lemon juice and sugar.

- Break the eggs into a bowl with a little salt and beat.

- Peel the prawns and cut them open at the back.

- Put the cooking oil in a wok on a medium heat.

- Dip each prawn in the egg, then cover with breadcrumbs.

- Then cook the prawns in the oil for a few minutes until they become a light gold colour.

- To make the lemon sauce, mix the lemon juice and palm sugar in a pan on medium heat and stir for 4–5 minutes until it becomes sticky.

- Serve the prawns onto plates. drip the lemon sauce on the top of the prawns and put lemon slices on the side of the plates as you serve.

Chicken with Coconut
Toam ka kai

- Put the coconut cream and salt in a wok on a medium heat and stir for 5 minutes.

- Add the lemongrass and galangal and cook for a further 3 minutes.

- Add the chicken pieces and cook for a further 15 minutes.

- Add the fish sauce and lemon juice.

- Serve sprinkled with chillies and coriander.

4 cups coconut cream

1 tsp salt

2 lemongrass stalks, white part only, cut into 5cm strips

1 galangal clove, sliced or broken into pieces

500g chicken breast meat, thinly sliced

2 tbsp fish sauce

5 tbsp lemon juice (or more to strengthen the flavour)

To garnish

1–5 small chillies, chopped

1 tbsp chopped fresh coriander

Galangal-Ka

Seafood with Coconut
Toam ka taray

500g mixed sea food, such as prawn, squid and mussel

4 cups coconut cream

1 tsp salt

2 lemongrass stalks, white part only, cut into 5cm pieces

1 galangal clove, sliced or broken into pieces

2 tbsp fish sauce

5 tbsp lemon juices (or more to taste)

To garnish
1–5 small chillies, chopped

1 tbsp chopped fresh coriander, for sprinkling

- ◆ Soak the prepared seafood in hot water for a few minutes, then drain.

- ◆ Put the coconut cream and salt in a wok pot on a medium heat and stir for 5 minutes.

- ◆ Add the lemongrass and galangal and continue cooking for 3 more minutes.

- ◆ Add the seafood and cook for 5–6 minutes.

- ◆ Add the fish sauce and lemon juice.

- ◆ Serve sprinkled with chillies and coriander.

Prawns with Straw Mushrooms
Toam yum koong

SERVES 4

- Remove prawn shells, cut open along to the tail and keep all the heads for stock.

- Put the water in a pan and bring to the boil on a medium heat.

- Add the prawn heads with the salt and cook for 5 minutes to make a stock. Strain and remove the prawn heads from the pot.

- Add the lemongrass, galangal, prawns, chillies and mushrooms and cook for 3 minutes.

- Add the fish sauce, lemon juice and kaffir lime leaves. Taste to make sure the taste is a bit sour and spicy.

- Serve sprinkled with coriander.

16 medium-sized prawns

5 cups water

1 tsp salt

2 lemongrass stalks, white part only, cut into 5cm long pieces

4 pieces galangal

3–5 small chillies, crushed with a large knife

100g straw mushrooms, halved

2–3 tbsp fish sauce

4 tbsp lemon juice

4 kaffir lime leaves

To garnish
8 sprigs of fresh coriander, chopped

kaffir lime

Stir-fried Noodles with Prawns
Paad Thai koong

4 tbsp fish sauce

4 tbsp palm sugar

1kg small sticky rice noodles

¼ cup cooking oil

1 piece of hard tofu, cut into small slices

2–3 garlic cloves, chopped

12 prawns, peeled and sliced open along the back

4 eggs

4 tbsp lemon juice

1 cup beansprouts

100g *koo chai*, cut into pieces about 5cm long

1 tbsp snipped fresh chives

¼ cup roasted peanuts, finely ground

Koo chai is a green vegetable like a spring onion, which can be used as an alternative if you cannot find any.

- Boil the fish sauce with the palm sugar for 5 minutes.

- Soak the noodles in water until soft.

- Heat the cooking oil in a wok on high heat until hot.

- Add the tofu and garlic and stir for 3 minutes.

- Add the prawns and cook for a few minutes until well done.

- Next add the 4 eggs and stir for 3 minutes.

- Drain the noodles, then add them to the wok, stir and mix well with fish sauce and sugar, lemon juice and beansprouts.

- Add the *koo chai*, heat through, then serve garnished with chives and peanuts.

Fried Noodles with Chicken

Koay teaw paad se eiw kai

SERVES 4

¼ cup cooking oil

300g chicken breast, thinly sliced

500g Chinese kale, cut into pieces 5–7cm long

1 tbsp chopped garlic

1kg flat rice noodles

3 tbsp sweet soy sauce

¼ cup soy sauce

- Warm the pan on a high heat, add the cooking oil and heat.

- When it is hot, add the chicken, kale and garlic, break in the eggs and stir for 3 minutes on medium heat.

- Mix the noodles with the sweet soy sauce, then stir into the pan with the soy sauce and cook for 3–5 more minutes until mixed well.

- Serve. *So easy!*

Tamarind fruit

Noodles with Meat Sauce

Kouy teaw nour sub

1kg flat noodles

¼ cup cooking oil

500g minced beef

1 tbsp chopped garlic

¼ cup chopped tomatoes

¼ cup soy sauce

3 tbsp sweet soy sauce

3 tbsp tomato sauce

1 tsp sugar

1 cup water

3 tbsp cornflour mixed with ¼ cup water

- On a medium heat, stir-fry the noodles for a few minutes with some of cooking oil. Keep to one side.

- To make the meat sauce, heat the oil in a wok on a medium heat.

- Add the minced meat, garlic and chopped tomatoes and stir for 3 minutes.

- Add the soy sauce, sweet soy sauce, tomato sauce and sugar and stir for 3 more minutes.

- Add the water and the cornflour and water to the sauce and stir briefly; the sauce will quickly turn a bit sticky.

- Pour the meat sauce on the noodles and serve with the lettuce.

Spicy Egg Noodles
Bamee paad ped

SERVES 4

- On a medium heat, add the cooking oil, garlic and chillies to the wok and stir for a few minutes.

- Add the prawns, mushrooms, soy sauce, water and sugar. Stir for 3–5 minutes until well cooked.

- Add the egg noodles and basil leaves and continue stirring until well mixed.

- Serve at once.

¼ cup cooking oil

1 tbsp chopped garlic

2–3 tbsp large chillies, chopped

300g prawns, cut and opened along the back

300g fresh straw mushroom or button mushrooms

¼ cup soy sauce

¼ cup water

2 tbsp sugar

1kg fresh egg noodles

1–3 sprigs of fresh basil leaves

Buddha Ayutthaya

Fried Mushroom with Prawns
Paad hed kaab koong

SERVES 4

5 tbsp cooking oil

3 garlic cloves, finely chopped

500g any fresh mushrooms, finely chopped

¼ cup water

3–5 tsp soy sauce

2 spring onions, cut into 5cm long pieces

300g medium prawns, shelled and veins removed

To serve
Steamed rice (page 19)

- Add the cooking oil to the wok and put on a medium heat until heated.

- Add the garlic and stir for 1 minute.

- Add the mushroom, water, soy sauce and spring onions and stir-fry for 3 minutes until well cooked.

- Add the prawns and stir for a few minutes until cooked.

- Transfer to serving plates and serve hot with steamed rice.

Garlic

Duck with Beansprouts
Paad ped kab tou ngok

- Add the cooking oil and garlic to a wok and stir on medium heat for 3–4 minutes.

- Add the duck, soy sauce and water and stir-fry for 2 minutes.

- Add the mushrooms and spring onions and stir-fry for 3 minutes.

- Add the beansprouts and stir-fry for 1–3 minutes until hot.

- Serve with steamed rice.

SERVES 4

¼ cup cooking oil

3–4 garlic cloves, chopped

500g skinless duck breast, thinly sliced

¼ cup soy sauce

¼ cup water

200g straw mushrooms, halved

2 bunches of spring onions, cut into 5cm long strips

500g beansprouts

To serve
Steamed rice (page 19)

Thai Shadow Puppet

1kg tender pork with
fat and skin, cut into
2.5cm cubes

4–6 tbsp soy sauce

4–5 garlic cloves,
chopped

½ tsp ground black
pepper

2 coriander roots,
finely chopped

¼ cup cooking oil

¼ cup fish sauce

¼ cup palm sugar

To garnish
5–8 coriander leaves

To serve
Steamed rice
(page 19)

Sweet Pork
Moo waan

This dish is sweet and salty and can be served with a
spicy curry if you wish.

- Put the pork, soy sauce, garlic, pepper and
  coriander roots in a bowl, mix well and leave for 10
  minutes.

- Add the cooking oil to the wok and turn to medium
  heat till the pan is hot.

- Add the pork mixture and stir-fry for 3 minutes.

- Add the fish sauce and palm sugar and continue to
  stir-fry, now cooking at a low heat, for 30 minutes,
  ensuring the pork and sauce are well mixed.

- During cooking, if the pork becomes dry, add the
  ¼ cup water a little at a time.

- Spoon on to large plates, garnish with coriander
  leaves and serve with steamed rice.

Fried Noodles with Vegetables

Kouy teaw paad pak roam

SERVES 4

½ cup cooking oil

1kg *kalian* (Chinese broccoli), thinly sliced

¼ cup sweet soy sauce to mix with noodles

¼ cup soy sauce

1kg fresh large rice noodles, cut into 1cm long pieces

500g beansprouts

2 tsp chilli powder (optional)

Tabasco sauce (optional)

- Add the cooking oil to the wok on medium heat, stir in the vegetables and stir-fry for 3 minutes.

- Stir the sweet soy sauce into the noodles, add to the pan and stir-fry for a further 3 minutes, adding the soy sauce during cooking.

- Add the beansprouts and cook for 1–3 minutes until hot.

- Spoon on to serving plates. If you wish, you can sprinkle with the chilli powder or Tabasco sauce as you serve.

Thai Orchid

11

Grilled and Deep-fried

Tamarind fruit

1 cup cooking oil

4 eggs

Deep-fried Eggs
Kgai dow

A simple thing here, but it goes so well with chicken dishes and the taste blends well with basil.

- On high heat, add the cooking oil to the wok and heat for 30 seconds, then turn down to medium heat.

- Break one egg into the wok and deep-fry both sides until a medium gold colour.

- Move the cooked egg to the plate and cook the other eggs in the same way.

Grilled Prawns with Honey Sauce

Koong yang naam poeng

SERVES 4

Before you start, soak some bamboo skewers in water for an hour or so to help prevent them from burning during grilling, as you would for satay.

* Mix all the sauce ingredients in a bowl.

* Add the prawns to the honey sauce, cover and leave for 1 hour in the fridge.

* Thread the prawns on to the skewers and grill or barbecue at medium heat for about 15 minutes, turning regularly to make sure they don't burn!

* Transfer to serving plates and serve with a mixed salad or grilled sweet corn.

2kg large prawns, peeled and slit down the back

For the honey sauce
½ cup honey

1 tsp yellow curry powder

1 tsp salt

2 tbsp lemon juice

To serve
Mixed salad or grilled sweetcorn

Prawns with Tamarind Sauce

Koong tod makarm

SERVES 4

50g tamarind pulp

1 cup water

1½ cups water

12 large prawns

2 cups cooking oil

5 red shallots, thinly sliced

1 sprigs of fresh coriander, leaves only

2–4 tbsp fish sauce

½ cup palm sugar

2 tbsp chopped fresh coriander

This is a great prawn dish with a sweet and sour flavour. Add a little more palm sugar if you like things sweet.

To make 1½ cups tamarind juice

- To make the tamarind juice, soak 50g of tamarind pulp in 1 cup water for 30 minutes until soft, squeeze by hand, then strain off the juice. You will need 1 ½ cups tamarind juice.

- Open the prawns along the back but do not peel (no need unless you want to).

- Add the cooking oil to the wok on a high heat and stir-fry the red shallots for a minute until they become light gold in colour. Remove from the wok.

- Reduce the heat to low, add the prawns and deep-fry for 3–5 minutes until they become gold in colour. Remove from the wok and keep warm.

- Now make the tamarind sauce. Leave about 3 tbsp cooking oil in the wok and put on a medium heat. Add the fish sauce, tamarind juice and palm sugar. Stir and cook until the sauce is sticky; this takes maybe 3–5 minutes.

- Pour the sauce to cover all the prawns, sprinkle with the fried shallots and some coriander and it's ready to serve.

Grilled Chicken
Kai yang

- Mix the chicken with all the other ingredients in the bowl.

- Grill the chicken in a hot oven at 200°C/gas 6 or on a barbecue for 20 minutes.

- Serve with the Thai dipping sauce.

SERVES 4

2kg chicken breast

½ cup coconut cream

1 tsp salt

1 tsp ground pepper

¼ cup soy sauce

To serve
Thai dipping sauce (page 20)

Tamarind fruit

500g medium-sized shrimps, shelled

¼ cup pork meat fat

1 tbsp red curry paste (page 24)

½ tbsp salt

3 cups cooking oil

100g wing beans or snake beans, very thinly sliced

For the dipping sauce
½ cup sugar

¼ cup rice vinegar

1 tbsp roasted peanuts

4 small cucumbers, cut into long, thin slices

3 shallots, finely chopped

1 large red chilli, thinly sliced

To garnish
2–3 fresh coriander leaves

Shrimp Cake
Tod maan koong

This can also be served with steamed rice (page 19) if you prefer.

- Mix the shrimps and the pork meat fat, then stir in the red curry paste and salt, blending until smooth.

- Make small, flat balls of the shrimp mince about 5cm in diameter.

- To make the sauce, add the sugar and vinegar to the pan, stirring on low heat until the sugar has dissolved, then boil for 3 minutes. Remove from the heat and allow to cool.

- Add the cucumbers, shallots and chillies. Place in a bowl and sprinkle with the coriander.

- Now heat the oil in a non-stick wok on a medium heat for 3 minutes.

- Add the shrimp balls and deep-fry for a few minutes until they turn a light gold colour.

- Lift out of the pan and drain off any excess oil on kitchen paper before serving.

- Serve piping hot with the dipping sauce.

Deep-fried Fish with Soya Bean Sauce
Pla tod toa jeaw

Use any white fish if you cannot buy white snapper.

- Prepare the fillets from the fish, keeping the tail intact.

- Make the soya bean sauce. Add 3 tbsp cooking oil to the wok on a medium heat. Stir in the garlic, soya beans, fish sauce, palm sugar and water. Cook, stirring, for 3–5 minutes until the sauce becomes sticky.

- Add the ginger and spring onions, then remove from the heat.

- Now add all the cooking oil to the wok and heat on a high heat for a moment.

- Turn to a medium heat and add the fish, making sure the cooking oil covers the whole fish (if not, you can add a little more). Cook for a few minutes until both sides of the fish are golden brown and crisp – that's for about 3–5 minutes (be careful not to let it get too hot and burn).

- Lift the fish out of the oil and drain on kitchen paper, then transfer to the plate, Pour the sauce over the fish, garnish the plate with red chillies and serve with steamed rice.

SERVES 4

4 cups cooking oil

4 x 500g white snapper

2–3 garlic cloves, chopped

3 tbsp soy beans

¼ cup fish sauce

2 tbsp palm sugar

1 cup water

1 cup thinly sliced fresh root ginger

3 spring onions, cut into 5cm inch long pieces

To garnish
2 long red chillies, thinly sliced

To serve
Steamed rice (page 19)

2kg pork, cut into
large thin pieces

3 litres or so of water
(enough to cover the
pork)

1 cup soy sauce

½ cup sugar

Crispy Pork
Moo yong

The crispy pork prepared this way makes a great snack for
all the family; you can eat it while watching television with
a drink – very tasty and good for you too.

- Bring the water to the boil in a pan on a high heat.

- Add the pork and cook on a low heat for 1 hour
  until the pork is tender.

- Remove the pork from the pan and cut or tear the
  pork along the grain into thin strips.

- Add the pork strips to the wok and cook on a
  medium heat for 3 minutes.

- Add the soy sauce and sugar and stir all the time for
  20 minutes.

- Continue cooking, stirring on a low heat for a
  further 30 minutes until the pork becomes light gold
  and crispy.

- If you do not want to eat at once, cool for couple of
  minutes before storing in an airtight jar or container
  until needed.

Curries

Thai Elephant figurine

Green Beef Curry
Gang keaw wan nour

SERVES 4

- ◆ On a medium heat, stir ½ cup of the thick coconut cream with the curry paste in the pan for 5 minutes, being careful not to let it get too dry.

- ◆ Add more coconut cream a little at a time, and cook until the curry sauce is an oily red colour.

- ◆ Now add the beef, the rest of the coconut cream, the fish sauce and palm sugar, stir and cook for 20 minutes until the beef is ready.

- ◆ Add the aubergine, basil leaves and chillies, stir well and serve.

4 cups coconut cream

1 tbsp green curry paste (page 22)

1 kg beef, thinly sliced

3–5 tbsp fish sauce

1 tbsp palm sugar

½ cup small aubergines, diced

½ cup sweet basil leaves

2–3 large chilli, thinly sliced

81

4 cups coconut cream

1 tbsp red curry paste
(page 24)

12 medium prawns

2–3 tbsp fish sauce

1 tbsp palm sugar

To garnish

3–5 kaffir lime leaves,
thinly sliced

1–2 red long chillies,
thinly sliced

Prawn Curry
Panang koong

- On a medium heat, add ¼ cup of the coconut
  cream to a wok and stir in the curry paste for a few
  minutes until the colour is an oily red.

- Add the remaining coconut cream a little at a time,
  maybe ¼ cup more, to prevent the curry sauce
  becoming too dry.

- Add the prawns and cook for 5 minutes.

- Add a little more coconut cream just to cover the
  prawns but you may not need all of it. This curry
  must be a bit dry with a sticky sauce rather than a
  normal curry.

- Add the fish sauce and palm sugar and cook for 3–4
  minutes.

- Spoon on to the plates, sprinkling with kaffir
  lime leaves and sliced chillies to make it ready for
  serving.

chilli

Chicken Curry
Panang kai

- On a medium heat, add ¼ cup of the coconut cream and stir in the curry paste for a few minutes until the colour is an oily red.

- Add the remaining coconut cream a little at a time, maybe ¼ cup more, to prevent the curry sauce becoming too dry.

- Add the chicken and cook for 5 minutes.

- Add a little more coconut cream just to cover the chicken but you may not need to use all of it. This curry must be a bit dry with a sticky sauce rather than a normal curry.

- Add the fish sauce and palm sugar and cook for 3–4 minutes.

- Spoon on to the plates, sprinkling with kaffir lime leaves and sliced chillies to make it ready for serving.

SERVES 4

4 cups coconut cream

1 tbsp red curry paste (page 24)

1kg chicken breast, diced

2–3 tbsp fish sauce

1 tbsp palm sugar

To garnish

3–5 kaffir lime leaves, thinly sliced

1–2 red long chillies, thinly sliced

coconut

1 cup aubergine, cut into bite-sized pieces

2 kg chicken breast

2kg coconut milk

2–4 tbsp green curry paste (page 22)

½ cup fish sauce

2 tbsp palm sugar

1 cup sweet basil leaves

2 red spur chillies, finely shredded

To serve
Steamed rice (page 19)

Green Chicken Curry
Kang keaw wan kai

This is a classic Thai dish. The curry is not too strong – *mai pet* – but can be made hotter if you want. This, like so many Thai dishes, is most usually served with rice, but I'll stop saying that every time.

- Put the aubergine in water to soak.

- Cut the chicken into long, thin strips.

- First, place the wok on a medium heat and add only ½ cup of the coconut milk with the curry paste. Fry the curry paste for a few minutes until it is shiny and coloured.

- Then gradually add the coconut milk a little at a time until the curry smells fragrant. Yes, smell is a good judge here.

- Add the chicken and cook for about 20 minutes until it becomes tender.

- Add the fish sauce and palm sugar, stir and taste to check the flavour.

- Drain the aubergine, add to the wok and cook for just a short time, adding a few sweet basil leaves and chilli to taste.

- Done: it's ready to enjoy.

Chicken and Potato Curry
Massaman kai

This is a well-known dish and it shows how changing the exact ingredients can alter a dish. I like to add the tamarind juice; my grandmother never did – both make a tasty dish!

- Cook the curry paste on a medium heat for a minute or two, then stir in about ½ cup thick coconut cream and continue to stir for 5 minutes, gradually adding more coconut cream as you do so, little by little, until the sauce is an oily red colour.

- Add the chicken and stir in the remainder of the coconut cream, then cook for 15 minutes.

- Add the potatoes, fish sauce, palm sugar and tamarind juice and stir well, then continue to cook the curry for about 30 minutes on a low heat until the chicken is well cooked and ready to serve.

SERVES 4

2 tbsp massaman curry paste (page 21)

6 cups coconut cream

1kg chicken breast, cut into 2.5cm thick pieces

2 large potatoes, peeled and cut into chunks

½ cup fish sauce

1–2 tbsp palm sugar

½ tbsp tamarind juice

Tamarind fruit

Pineapple Curry with Prawns

Kang sabprarod koong

4 cups coconut cream

1 tbsp red curry paste (page 24)

300g prawns, peeled, heads removed and cut open down the back

1 medium-sized pineapple, peeled and chopped into long, thin pieces

2–3 tbsp fish sauce

- Warm the pan on medium heat.

- Add about ¼ cup of the coconut cream, stir in the curry paste cook for a few minutes until the colour is an oily red.

- Add the remaining coconut cream, the prawns, pineapple and fish sauce and cook for 20 minutes before serving.

Pineapple

Red Beef Curry
Panang nour

SERVES 4

- On a medium heat, add ¼ cup of the coconut cream and stir in the curry paste for a few minutes until the colour is an oily red.

- Add the remaining coconut cream a little at a time, maybe ¼ cup more, to prevent the curry sauce becoming too dry.

- Add the prawns and cook for 5 minutes.

- Add a little more coconut cream just to cover the prawns but you may not need all of it. This curry must be a bit dry with a sticky sauce rather than a normal curry.

- Add the fish sauce and palm sugar and cook for 3–4 minutes.

- Spoon on to the plates, sprinkling with kaffir lime leaves and sliced chillies to make it ready for serving.

4 cups coconut cream

1 tbsp red curry paste (page 24)

12 medium prawns

2–3 tbsp fish sauce

1 tbsp palm sugar

To garnish

3–5 kaffir lime leaves, thinly sliced

1–2 red long chillies, thinly sliced

400g tender beef

2–4 cups cooking oil

1 tbsp red curry paste
(page 24)

2 tbsp fish sauce

¼ cup water

1 tsp sugar

To garnish
5 kaffir lime leaves,
thinly sliced

Stir-fried Beef Curry
Nour paad prik

- Cut the beef into thin slices.

- On a medium heat, add the cooking oil to the wok.
  Add the curry paste and stir for 30 seconds.

- Add the meat together with the fish sauce, water
  and sugar. Cook, stirring, for about 10 minutes until
  the meat is well done.

- Serve on to the plates, sprinkling with the kaffir
  lime leaves.

kaffir lime

Snake Bean
with Prawns
Tou faak yao paad prik koong

You can buy snake beans in Asian stores, or substitute green beans or sugar snap peas if you can't find them.

- On a medium heat, add the cooking oil to the wok and stir in the curry paste for 30 seconds.

- Add the prawns and cook for 2 minutes.

- Add the snake beans and water, fish sauce and sugar, stirring for 5 minutes until well done.

- Serve sprinkled with kaffir lime leaves to finish off.

2–4 cups cooking oil

1 tbsp red curry paste (page 24)

8 medium-sized prawns, cut open at back leaving the tail

500g snake beans, cut into 5cm long pieces

¼ cup water

2 tbsp fish sauce

1 tsp sugar

To garnish
5 kaffir lime leaves, very thinly sliced

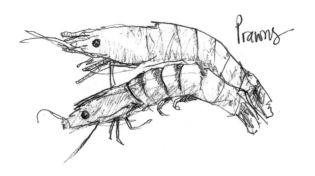

Prawns

Massaman Beef Curry
Massaman nour

2 tbsp massaman curry paste (page 21)

4 cups coconut cream

1kg beef, cut into 2.5cm thick pieces

2 large potatoes, cut into chunks

½ cup fish sauce

1–2 tbsp palm sugar

½ tbsp tamarind juice

You can also buy massaman curry paste at Asian stores.

- Cook the curry paste on a medium heat, adding about ½ cup thick coconut cream and stirring for 30 seconds.

- Stir the coconut and curry paste for 5 minutes, gradually adding more coconut cream as you do so, little by little, until the sauce is an oily red colour.

- Add the beef, stir in the remainder of the coconut cream and cook for 15 minutes.

- Add the potatoes, the fish sauce, palm sugar and tamarind juice and stir well. Cook the curry for about 30 minutes on a low heat until the beef is well cooked and ready to serve.

Fillet of Fish with Curry Sauce
Panang pla

SERVES 4

¼ cup cooking oil

4 fish fillets

2 cups coconut cream

1 tbsp red curry paste (page 24)

2 tbsp fish sauce

1 tbsp palm sugar

To garnish

4 large red chillies cut into long slices.

1–3 leaves sweet basil

* Add the cooking oil to a non-stick pan and place on medium heat until hot.

* Add the 4 pieces of fish and cook, turning occasionally, until they are light gold on both sides.

* Meanwhile, make the curry sauce. Add the coconut cream to a separate pan on a medium heat and stir until hot.

* Add the curry paste and stir for 3 minutes.

* Add the fish sauce and palm sugar and stir for 3 more minutes until the curry sauce is sticky.

* Serve the fish on to plates and pour the sauce over the top, then garnish with the chillies and sweet basil leaves on the top.

Thai Shadow Puppet

4 cups coconut cream

1 tbsp red curry paste
(page 24)

½ cup shrimps

3 tbsp fish sauce, or to
taste

1 tbsp palm sugar

500g mushrooms

¼ cup basil leaves

2 long red chillies,
thinly sliced

To serve
Steamed rice
(page 19)

Mushroom Curry
Kang ped hed

I like to use straw mushrooms, but you can use any kind
for this dish.

- Add ¼ cup coconut cream to the wok on medium
  heat. Stir in the curry paste for a few minutes until
  it is an oily red colour.

- Gradually add the remaining coconut cream, with
  the shrimps, fish sauce and palm sugar and cook for
  about 3–4 minutes.

- Add the mushrooms, basil leaves and chillies, and
  continue cooking for a further 3 minutes.

- Remove from the heat, serve with steamed rice.

chilli

Roasted Duck Curry
Gang ped yang

- Add ¼ cup of the coconut cream to a wok on medium heat and stir with the curry paste until it is an oily red colour. During this time, add some more of the coconut cream if the curry sauce is dry.

- Add the remaining coconut cream together with the duck breast, fish sauce and sugar and cook for 15 minutes.

- Add the lychees and basil leaves, remove from the heat and garnish with the red chillies.

- Serve with steamed rice.

SERVES 4

4 cups coconut cream

2 tbsp red curry paste (page 24)

1kg roasted duck breast, thinly sliced

3 tbsp fish sauce

1 tbsp palm sugar

100g lychees, shelled

1–2 sprigs of sweet basil leaves

To garnish

2 long red chillies, thinly sliced

To serve

Steamed rice (page 19)

Lychees

Tofu Curry with Pineapple

Kang toahu sabprarod

4 cups coconut cream

1 tbsp red curry paste
(page 24)

2 x 250g cakes of firm
tofu, cut into cubes

1 pineapple, peeled
and finely chopped

¼ cup soy sauce

To serve
Steamed rice
(page 19)

- Add ¼ cup of the coconut cream to the wok on a medium heat and stir with the curry paste until it becomes an oily red colour.

- Add the tofu, pineapple, the rest of the coconut cream and the soy sauce and then cook for 15 minutes.

- Serve with steamed rice.

Pineapple

Thai Vegetarian Dishes

In Thailand every October there is an old, largely Chinese, tradition of serving vegetarian dishes; you notice this especially in Bangkok's China Town and in Phuket, where there are big celebrations – any excuse for a food festival is taken in Thailand! The next few recipes here – *aharn je* – are included as they are typical of what might be served.

Cold Cut Tofu
Toa hu yen

SERVES 4

2 x 250g packs tofu

4 tbsp soy sauce

2 bunches of spring onions, thinly sliced

This dish makes a tasty appetiser.

* Cut the bean curd into 2.5cm cubes and arrange on serving plates.
* Sprinkle each one with soy sauce and garnish with spring onion.

Fried Mixed Vegetables
Paad paak roam

2 cups finely chopped
broccoli

2 cups snow peas
(mangetout)

2 cups finely chopped
carrots

1 cup baby corn

Salt

¼ cup cooking oil

¼ cup soy sauce

3 tbsp sesame oil

¼ cup water

To serve

Steamed rice
(page 19)

- ◆ Bring a pan of salted water to the boil. Add all the vegetables and blanch for 2 minutes, then transfer to cold water to stop the cooking process, then drain well.

- ◆ Add the cooking oil to a wok and cook on a medium heat until hot.

- ◆ Add all the vegetables, the soy sauce and sesame oil and stir for 3 minutes, gradually adding the water as you stir.

- ◆ Serve on plates with steamed rice.

Fried Aubergine with Soya Beans

Paad makour yao kaab toa jeaw

SERVES 4

½ cup cooking oil

1kg long aubergines, thinly sliced

500g small tomatoes, quartered

½ cup water

2 tbsp soy beans

½ cup sweet basil leaves

2 large red chillies, thinly sliced

To serve
Steamed rice
(page 19)

- Add the cooking oil to the wok on a medium heat and when it is hot, add the aubergines and tomatoes and stir-fry for a few minutes until soft.

- Add the water, soy beans and basil leaves, and stir for a few more minutes.

- Garnish with chillies and serve with steamed rice.

Thai Pea Aubergines

Mixed Vegetable Stew
Toam jaab chai

½ cup cooking oil

1kg cabbage, thinly sliced

2 cups carrots, thinly sliced

2 cups baby corns

1 cup of small tomatoes, thinly sliced

Water to cover

½ cup soy sauce

200g fresh mushroom, thinly sliced

To serve
Steamed rice (page 19)

- ◆ Heat the cooking oil in a wok over a high heat until hot, then add the cabbage, carrots, corn and tomatoes and stir-fry for 5 minutes.

- ◆ Transfer to a pan and add enough water to cover. Add the soy sauce and mushrooms and cook, now on a low heat, for 1 hour.

- ◆ Serve with steamed rice.

benjarong bowl

Thai Omelette with Tomatoes and Onion

Kgai jeuw makourtes huahom

Omelette seems like a simple dish – indeed it is – but make no mistake, the flavour of Thai omelette is not like European style – it is very tasty. It can be a meal in itself or accompany other food.

- Heat the cooking oil in a wok over a medium heat.
- Beat the eggs with the water.
- Mix the tomato and onion into the eggs and pour the mixture into the wok, together with the soy sauce. Add the spring onion if you like.
- Cook the eggs for a few minutes, allowing them to set and become a little crispy at the edges.
- Serve with steamed rice.

SERVES 4

¼ cup cooking oil

4 eggs

2 tbsp water

1 large tomato, sliced or chopped

½ small onion, finely chopped

1 tsp soy sauce

A little spring onion, finely chopped (optional)

To serve
Steamed rice (page 19)

14

1 cup pancake flour

½–1 cup milk

2 cups cooking oil

1 tbsp tempura flour
(*koki*)

4 bananas, peeled
and cut into 5 pieces

For sprinkling
1–2 tbsp icing sugar

½ cup honey

Desserts

Deep-fried Banana
Klouy hom tod

Instant ready-mixed pancake flour and tempura flour can be bought in Asian stores.

- Whisk pancake flour and half the milk in a bowl to make a batter. Gradually add enough of the remaining milk to give the right consistency – not too thick.

- Warm up a non-stick pan, add the cooking oil on a high heat and cook until hot, then turn down to medium heat.

- Toss the banana pieces in the tempura flour, one by one, using a tablespoon, so they are coated with flour. Then dip them in the batter.

- Deep-fry the banana pieces for just a few minutes until they fluff up like small balls and turn a light gold colour.

- Serve sprinkled with a little icing sugar and honey.

Tapioca with Dried Black Bean Sauce

Tom tou dam

This is a popular kind of Thai dessert that is easy and quick to make. Note that you can add the young coconut to the tapioca during cooking *'to make more tasty'* – see what you like best.

SERVES 4

2 cups dried black beans

4 cups coconut cream

2 cups sugar

1 cup tapioca

4 cups water

½ tsp salt

- Add the black beans to a pot with the coconut cream and cook on a medium heat until black beans are soft, about 10 minutes.

- Add 1 cup of the sugar and cook for a further 3 minutes.

- Add the tapioca and water to the pot with the remaining sugar and the salt, and boil for 5 minutes, stirring all the time.

- Remove from the heat.

- Serve the tapioca hot in small bowls and add the black beans and coconut cream on the top.

½ cup coconut cream

½ tsp salt

4 cups water

1 cup sticky rice, soaked in boiling water

1 cup corn kernels

¾ cup sugar

Sticky Rice with Corn
Koa neaw peak koa poad

You can also make this with tofu, in which case, dice it and add it with the sticky rice.

- Heat the coconut cream on a low heat until warm, then add the salt and stir. Keep the cream warm.

- Heat the water In a separate pan, Drain the sticky rice, add to the pan and cook on a medium heat for 20–30 minutes.

- Add the corn and sugar and cook until sticky rice is well cooked. If it becomes dry, add a little more water.

- Serve hot, with the coconut cream poured on the top.

Pumpkin with Coconut
Gang boach phak tong

SERVES 4

500g pumpkin

4 cups coconut cream

1 cup palm sugar

½ tsp salt

- Peel the skin off the pumpkin, remove the seeds and cut the flesh into small cubes. Rinse in cold water.

- Reserve 3 tbsp of the coconut cream for decoration. Put the remainder in a pan and cook on medium heat, stirring all the time, until hot.

- Next add the pumpkin and cook for about 5 minutes until medium-soft.

- Add the sugar and cook for a further 3 minutes.

- Add the salt and serve while hot with a spoonful of coconut cream on the top, just for decoration.

Coconut

Conversion charts

All the recipes are set out with measures for four people, though this can, of course, be varied as you wish for larger or smaller portions and more or fewer people.

I use a cup for measuring. 1 cup = 250ml of liquid, or whatever volume fits into the space, so the same weight of two different foods – butter and flour, for example, will have different cup measurements. You can use a set of American-style cup measures, which are readily available, or a traditional English cup (tiny variances are not significant) or use an ordinary measuring jug.

If you prefer to use imperial measures or weights, you can use these conversions.

Weight				
Metric	Imperial	US 100g = 1 cup	US 175g = 1 cup	US 225g = 1 cup
		Flour, nuts, breadcrumbs, etc.	Dried fruit, lentils, etc.	Butter, sugar, cream cheese, etc.
25g	1oz	¼ cup		1/8 cup
50g	2oz	½ cup		¼ cup
75g	3oz	2/3 cup	½ cup	1/3 cup
100g	4oz	1 cup		½ cup
150g	5oz	1 ¼ cups		2/3 cup
175g	6oz	1 ½ cups	1 cup	¾ cup
200g	7oz	1 ¾ cups		Scant 1 cup
225g	8oz	2 cups		1 cup
250g	9oz	2 ½ cups	1 ½ cups	1 1/8 cups
300g	10oz	2 ¾ cups		1 1/3 cups
350g	12oz	3 cups	2 cups	1 ½ cups
400g	14oz	3 ½ cups		1 2/3 cups
450g	1lb	4 cups	2 1/3 cups	2 cups

Liquids		
Metric	**Imperial**	**US cups**
5ml	1 tsp	1 tsp
15ml	1 tbsp	1 tbsp
50ml	2fl oz	3 tbsp
60ml	2 ½ fl oz	¼ cup
75ml	3fl oz	1/3 cup
100ml	4fl oz	scant ½ cup
125ml	4 ½ fl oz	½ cup
150ml	5fl oz	2/3 cup
200ml	7fl oz	scant 1 cup
250ml	10fl oz	1 cup
300ml	½pt	1 1/4 cups
350ml	12fl oz	1 1/3 cups
400ml	3/4pt	1 ¾ cups
500ml		2 cups
600ml	1pt	2 ½ cups

Oven temperatures	
Metric	**Imperial**
110°C	225°F
120°C	250°F
140°C	275°F
150°C	300°F
160°C	325°F
180°C	350°F
190°C	375°F
200°C	400°F
220°C	425°F
230°C	450°F
240°C	475°F

Measurements	
Metric	**Imperial**
5cm	2in
10cm	4in
13cm	5in
15cm	6in
18cm	7in
20cm	8in
25cm	10in
30cm	12in

Index

SOME OTHER TITLES FROM HOW TO BOOKS

MAKE YOUR OWN JELLIED PRESERVES
An easy guide to home and hedgerow jelly making
CAROLINE PAKENHAM

This book will show you how you can use the fruits and herbs you can grow in your garden, or the fruits that you can pick yourself from the hedgerows, to make into jars of delicious jelly preserves – quickly, easily, cheaply, and without fuss. It will enable even the true beginner to understand what to do, and feel confident and proud of their end product. The book includes full colour photos to help you recognise hedgerow fruits, plus numerous recipes for fruits that you can gather locally from spring to autumn or buy from further afield.

ISBN 978-1-905862-76-4

EAT WELL, SPEND LESS
The complete money-saving guide to everyday cooking
SARAH FLOWER

This invaluable book contains over 200 great family recipes for busy cooks who want to save time and money, but also deliver wholesome food for their families. It's also an essential housekeeper's guide for the 21st century. Nutritionist Sarah Flower shows you how to feed yourself and your family a healthy balanced diet without spending hours in the kitchen and a fortune in the supermarket.

ISBN 978-1-905862-83-2

THE EVERYDAY FISH COOKBOOK
Simple, delicious recipes for cooking fish
TRISH DAVIES

This book contains simple but delicious recipes for all the popular varieties of local fish as well as species from overseas – often more sustainable - that can be bought in fishmongers. Fish is high in protein, low in fat – and rich in nutrients. So it is a food we should be eating more of, and including regularly in our meals. The recipes in this book are approachable, flexible and uncomplicated, advising on buying, preparation, and freezing as well as cooking.

ISBN 978-1-905862-73-3

MAKING MEAD, CIDER, PERRY AND FRUIT WINES
Recipes, and how to make them
CRAIG HUGHES

This book will show you how to use honey, apples, pears and garden fruits to make alcoholic and non-alcoholic drinks that you can enjoy throughout the year.

There are many interesting drinks that have been lost to time, but some, such as cider, mead (which has been around since about 7000 BC) and perry are reinventing themselves. This book explains where and when to find your raw materials and what sort of equipment you'll need. It includes delicious recipes that use common and less common fruits.

ISBN 978-1-905862-82-5

HOW TO GROW YOUR OWN FRUIT AND VEG
A week-by-week guide to wild-life friendly fruit and vegetable gardening
JOE HASHMAN

'An absolute must for anyone serious about growing their own produce.'
Grow It!

Joe Hashman takes you outdoors and 'in amongst it' on the vegetable plot where seeds are sown, plants nurtured, fruits tended and crops harvested. With his guidance – and your gardening – your kitchen garden, vegetable patch or allotment will provide you with good, fresh, honest and seasonal fruit and vegetables.

ISBN 978-1-905862-77-1

PLANTS AND PLANTING PLANS FOR A BEE GARDEN
How to design your beds and borders to attract bees
MAUREEN LITTLE

This book will enable you to select bee-friendly plants, and to plan borders which are beneficial to bees, encouraging these most valuable of insects to come to your garden over and over again, both for sustenance and to aid pollination. It contains a wide range of practical, beautiful and easy to follow planting plans for bee-friendly gardens of all sizes, including: traditional mixed, cottage- and colour-themed borders; 'designer' and 'natural' borders; borders for acid and alkaline soils; ideas for container planting. It also includes over 180 colour illustrations.

ISBN 978-1-905862-80-1

MAKE & MEND
A guide to recycling clothes and fabrics
REBECCA PEACOCK AND SAM TICKNER

This book shows how, with a little knowledge and creativity, you can make a wide range of fantastic items from those old clothes and fabrics you can't bear to throw away. Whether it's a cushion cover from a coat, a tote bag from a torn dress or a neck tie from a negligee, this book will show you how to make it. Packed full of projects, from aprons to curtains, bags to jewellery, we show you how to turn a pile of scraps into wearable, beautiful and personalized items. Each project offers a step-by-step guide to making successful pieces.

ISBN 978-1-905862-79-5

How To Books are available through all good bookshops, or you can order direct from us through Grantham Book Services.

Tel: +44 (0)1476 541080
Fax: +44 (0)1476 541061

Or Via our website
www.howtobooks.co.uk

To order via any of these methods please quote the title(s) of the book(s) and your credit card number together with its expiry date.

For further information about our books and catalogue, please contact:

How To Books
Spring Hill House
Spring Hill Road
Begbroke
Oxford OX5 1RX

Visit our website at
www.howtobooks.co.uk

Or you can contact us by email at info@howtobooks.co.uk